DREAM
INTERPRETATION
Time to read your Mail

DREAM INTERPRETATION
Time to read your Mail

LAVAL W. BELLE

Noahs Ark Publishing Service
Beverly Hills, California

Dream Interpretation: Time to Read Your Mail

ISBN 979-8-9920102-7-5

Copyright © 2025 by Laval W. Belle

Published by:

Noahs Ark Publishing Service
8549 Wilshire Blvd., Suite 1442
Beverly Hills, CA 90211
www.noahsarkpublishing.com

Edited by Sharon Hogg & Carolyn Billups
Graphic Design by Keecia Henderson & Christopher C. White
Interior Design by Andrea Reider

Printed in the United States of America © 2025 All rights reserved. No part of this book may be reproduced or copied in any form without written permission from the author and/or publisher.

*God, I thank you for revealing Your dreams for me.
To my sister, Michelle Karen Belle,
thank you for supporting all of my dreams.*

TABLE OF CONTENTS

Introduction — ix

Chapter 1: Dreams — 1

Chapter 2: Visions — 5

Chapter 3: Meditation — 15

Chapter 4: Are You A Gifted Dreamer? — 21

Chapter 5: Dream Interpretation — 27

Chapter 6: Dream Interpretation Formula — 33

Chapter 7: 30-Day Dream Interpretation Journal — 45

INTRODUCTION

I cannot remember a time in my life when I did not experience dreams or visions. Dreaming, for me, is synonymous with breathing. Every major decision in my life involved consultation through dreams and visions.

We dream before we can speak. In our mother's womb we begin to store up images, sounds and feelings. Dreams and visions are older than time itself. The greatest personal trainers you will ever have are your dreams and visions.

As a child, I had many nightmares, along with some visions. I recall sitting in the classroom, staring off into space, picturing myself on a large stage playing drums. My spirit transported me to places and possibilities I never imagined would actually happen.

I am the sixth of ten children. My home was often crowded, confusing and most times absent of love and understanding. But I was comforted by my dreams and visions. Dreams and visions gave me hope and encouragement. Little by little, I discovered I could truly rely on my dreams and visions for guidance.

Dreams were my means of transporting myself to other worlds outside of my chaotic environment. As I got older, the dreams started to make more sense, and I started to rely on them for inspiration, guidance and protection.

I've discovered that dreams and visions are God's Divine Postal Service. Think about it— everyone has access to God's postal service. There is no cost for postage, shipping or handling. It's free! We never have to worry about divine mail getting lost or placed in the wrong mailbox. Like the natural postal service, sometimes we receive mail we don't understand, mail that seems to be in a different language, or news we just don't want to hear. When I dedicated my life to God, my dreams became much clearer, and I discovered the importance of dream language.

Through our natural parents, we mimic and learn to speak. We also instinctively learn to communicate spiritual language. But what good are dreams and visions if we cannot interpret them? How can we tell the difference between junk mail and important mail?

As a gifted dream interpreter, I've come to realize the importance and need for dream interpretation on every level. We live in a world of massive mail fraud and the business of misinformation. It's time to rediscover the importance of reading your own divine mail addressed to you from Heaven. All other mail, in my opinion, is secondary.

It's time to read your own Dreams and Visions—and stop reading the mail of others for inspiration. Dreams are a down payment on your future. Visions are the blueprints of your purpose.

I want to thank my friend, Dr. Hosea Collins, for encouraging me to "Get off your assets and write your second book on dreams and visions".

So, come on—let's open your dream mail today!

CHAPTER ONE

DREAMS

Dreams and visions are among the most intimate and fascinating encounters we will ever experience in life. They are our connection between the natural and thcipe supernatural. Everyone experiences some type of dream state. Every dream originates in the unseen realm. Not all dreams are divine, but all dreams have a functioning purpose.

The difference between dreams and visions is this: we encounter dreams while we are asleep, and visions while awake. I believe the brain—or the soul—is our supernatural mailbox. The brain plays a crucial role in initiating and regulating REM sleep, a stage characterized by rapid eye movements, muscle paralysis, and heightened brain activity.

It is my belief that dreams and visions operate in three basic categories:

1. **Divine** - The Kingdom of Heaven or The Spirit of Light
2. **Natural** - Communication processes within self; interaction between the conscious and subconscious mind. Example: dream content influenced by a combination of recent experiences, memories, emotions, and random neutral activity.
3. **Demonic** - The Kingdom of Darkness. the Spirit of Deception

While the world of dreams and visions is exciting, fearful, and fascinating, it is important to determine the source. Sometimes a dream can be a matter of life or death, freedom or bondage. I'm not trying to frighten you, but when a message is delivered from the Kingdom of Light or the Kingdom of Darkness, we need to take this correspondence seriously.

Think about it. On average, one-third of your life is spent in Dream World. It's important that you familiarize yourself with this divine postal system.

James, the half-brother of Jesus, said, "Every good gift and every perfect gift is from above and comes down from the Father of Lights." Everything, everyone, and every gift originates from God. Even nature, in all its glory, is the manifestation of God's unseen world.

I'm not trying to indoctrinate or proselytize you into some type of religion or philosophy. It's a fact that we live a two-tract existence: a seen world processed with our natural eyes, and an unseen world processed through our senses—like breathing air, hearing sounds, and feeling instinct.

James said that every gift comes from above. Anything above this immediate atmosphere is called heaven. He categorizes the first gift as good. The Greek word for good is "Agathos," which means benefit.

Dreams are gifts from God. Dream mail, gifted dreamers, and dream interpreters are divine gifts from heaven. Access to dreams and visions are available to everyone at no cost. These are inherited benefits.

James said there are perfect gifts. The word perfect in Greek is "Telelos." It means complete. A combination of other gifts, along with dreams and visions, makes our gifts complete.

Without the benefits of our dreams and visions, our abilities and resources are incomplete. The absence of dreams and visions is to function at two-thirds capacity.

Spiritual dreams and visions come from the Father through the vehicle of light. The Greek word for light is "Phao" (to shine or make manifest, especially by rays). A divine postal system is delivered through the power and speed of light. Light travels at approximately 186,232 miles per second. Wow! Now that's perfection!

We live in a rapidly changing world of communication. We have access to the internet, social media, and the ever-growing presence of AI. As fast as our information systems travel, it's important that we utilize all options.

Divine Inheritance

Dreams and visions are your divine inheritance. It is up to you whether or not you take advantage of them. They are the original means of communication and the language of heaven. Dreams and visions are God's personal letters to you and a resource that was never created for deception, ignorance or manipulation.

God often uses dreams to reveal His unique purpose for you. Such was the case with the Seer, Jeremiah. God communicated His purpose to Jeremiah when he was a teenager. Listen to what God said to this gifted Seer through a dream: "The word of the Lord came to me saying, 'Before I formed you in the womb I knew you. I ordained you.'"

As I shared with you earlier, dreams are older than time itself. We begin counting time when a baby is born. When a mother delivers her child, the clock starts. However, there are two previous trimesters in the developmental stages of human creation. The first trimester period begins in heaven. Jeremiah was a spiritual being before he was a natural being in his mother's womb. God divinely communicates with Jeremiah his complete history. The dream articulates Jeremiah's purpose was determined before he was born.

"Before you were born" reflects Jeremiah's second trimester. The second trimester is the orchestration of the body, soul, and spirit. It's the stage where we naturally develop our general sense of taste, touch, smell, hearing, and sight. The mother's womb is also where dreams and visions are incubated. It is where lifelong dream boxes are created.

We are born with direct access to heaven—no matter the race, religion, gender, or nationality. It is literally a divine inheritance. We have access to God's divine postal service. Dreams and visions do not discriminate. They are an equal service to everyone.

God informs Jeremiah, "Before you were born, I sanctified you." Sanctified means to cleanse or prepare. He goes on to say, "I ordained you a prophet to the nations." God explains Jeremiah's spiritual and natural trimesters; pre-womb (heaven), in the womb (developmental), and post womb (birth).

The inheritance of dreams and visions clearly originates in the divine. God has at His disposal all of creation to communicate His will through the medium of dreams and visions.

Finally, God encourages Jeremiah that He would put His words in Jeremiah's mouth. Amazing—there are many examples of how God communicates His purpose for us through dreams.

CHAPTER TWO

VISIONS

Vision is the ability to think about or plan the future with imagination or wisdom. It can also be an experience of seeing someone or something in a dream or trance as a supernatural apparition.

An **apparition** is a ghost-like image of a person—in other words, a spirit.

Keep in mind that dreams and visions are delivered by Divine Mail Carriers. Who are these mail carriers? Angels and spirits who provide revelation. Human Divine Mail Carriers include seers, prophets, gifted dreamers, and visionaries.

Other words for visions include trance, ideas, daydreams, and déjà vu.

A divine vision is God connecting images to His message. The difference between dreams and visions is that we experience dreams during an unconscious state (sleep), while visions occur during an altered conscious state (awake). Vision is seeing with the eyes of the Supernatural.

Dreams and visions are like motion pictures with sound. Metaphorically, a vision is a divine collaboration between a scriptwriter (dreamer), film writer (vision), and camera (mind).

Daniel, a gifted prophet, said to King Nebuchadnezzar, "Your dream, and the visions of your head upon your bed." The collaboration of the dream and vision is on full display in the story of a king searching for the meaning and interpretation of his dream vision.

Vision is the blueprint of purpose and conveys a clear picture that requires action.

DREAM INTERPRETATION

Habakkuk, a seer and musician, wrote these words after seeking guidance during a dark period of intense violence in the southern nation of Israel. This is the divine mail he received: "Write the vision."

As I shared in Chapter One, after we experience revelation, it is important to practice documentation. Just as important natural mail must be placed in a safe location so it is not lost or forgotten, the same approach should be taken when we download divine impartation. Document what you receive so it is not lost or forgotten.

Divine impartation is just as important as a birth certificate. Birth certificates are proof that you exist. Documentation is evidence that you experienced an encounter with Heaven's supernatural mail service.

Habakkuk's vision further communicates, "And Make It Plain On Tablets."

During that period, people wrote on tablets. Today, we have several dream documentation options—paper, digital notes, computer, sound recordings, pictures, and film. So, you have no excuse.

Documentation is a vital component in memorializing what you download from the spiritual realm.

Why is documentation so important? Pay attention to what Habakkuk said: "That he may run who reads it."

Dreams are seeds that inspire dialogue. Visions are blueprints that frequently require action.

Habakkuk encourages us, "For the vision is yet for an appointed time; but at the end it will speak, and it will not lie. Though it tarries, wait for it; because it will surely come, It will not tarry." Wow! What a comprehensive download.

Vision gives us a timetable. Visions are for an appointed time. Do not confuse an appointment with an assignment. Assignments are seasonal.

The vision instructs us to stay alert for continued mail. That is the perpetual inspiration of Habakkuk. Stick with the plan. Sometimes it feels like nothing is moving, but remain watchful and follow the instructions. A tree's roots grow downward to establish a strong foundation. Even though we cannot see the construction, the tree is growing—and so are your visions.

Solomon said, "Where there is no vision, the people perish." The word vision also means revelation. Stick to the vision.

Habakkuk's timeless lesson instructs us to listen, because at the end of the vision, the plan will speak for itself. Remember, dreams and visions are a collaboration. Natural filmmakers secure music composers to accompany what they see.

Visions are dramatic, so pay attention to the characters and details in the divine presentation. Habakkuk was informed that the vision "will not lie."

What should you do when your vision seems delayed? "Though it tarries, wait for it." Do not allow anxiety to rob you of your appointment and destiny. Your dreams and visions will happen.

God has uniquely customized a vision just for you. God created you in His divine image.

Visions are what we see, sense, and execute.

Like the natural postal system, we not only receive letters, but also postcards, magazines, pictures and digital mail. God imparts spiritual mail and packages through dreams and visions.

Glasses are worn to help us see clearly. You must wear supernatural lenses to read your spiritual mail.

Projected Vision

Paul encourages us to "walk by faith, not by sight." "Faith is the substance of things hoped for, the evidence of things not seen." Faith, metaphorically, is supernatural glasses.

The substance includes what you imagine in the supernatural realm. You can create with your imagination. The images are visible first to you.

Ideas are visions. Vision is the ability to think, create or plan through imagination.

My question is this: Are you exercising your endless resource of imagination?

Many people create vision boards—collages of images, words, and affirmations that visually represent goals and dreams. They inspire motivation and focus.

Vision boards serve as daily reminders of what you want to accomplish and function as tools for manifesting dreams.

Your imagination is available anytime, anywhere, regardless of circumstances.

Other tools that connect us to the spirit realm include affirmations and meditation, which I will discuss in greater detail in the next chapter.

DREAM INTERPRETATION

It's time to respond to your own vision mail. Start writing your visions on the tablet of your imagination and deposit them into your supernatural mailbox.

Your visions are on assignment. They are always working on your behalf.

When you are in a dream state, your mail should be read by you. When you entertain visions, it is time to take action on your divine mail.

The prophet Joel said, "It shall come to pass, your old men shall dream Dreams." Whether the dreamer acts on the dream or not, the message is still delivered.

Joel continues, "Your young men shall see visions." God makes a distinction between old and young. Vision is often assigned to the young to carry out the plan of God. Joel's prophecy is not fully manifested until the end of time.

Vision foretells the future—including technologies that did not exist during Joel's lifetime. Today, God is downloading dreams and visions indiscriminately, regardless of time, age, culture, gender, or religion.

I would like to introduce the most celebrated mail carrier from heaven—the angel Gabriel. Gabriel delivered a message to a teenage girl over 2,000 years ago that altered history.

Gabriel informed Mary that she was supernaturally pregnant and announced the child's name, "Jesus" (Yeshua). The Savior of the World—His name identified His mission.

I've explained the difference between dreams and visions, but sometimes we experience direct encounters with angels.

What Is an Encounter?

An encounter with the spiritual realm is a deeply personal experience—one involving a strong sense of divine intervention.

Joseph received his mail through dreams, and the carrier was unidentified—not so with Mary.

"The angel Gabriel was sent by God to a city of Galilee named Nazareth, to a virgin betrothed to a man whose name was Joseph. The virgin's name was Mary."

The characters are clearly identified as Joseph, Mary and the angel from Heaven. Pay attention to what follows.

VISIONS

"And having come in, the angel said to her, 'Rejoice, highly favored one, the Lord is with you; blessed are you among women.' But when she saw him, she was troubled, and considered what manner of greeting this was."

Scripture does not identify whether Mary was dreaming or awake. It simply states, "She saw Gabriel." She both saw and spoke with the angel.

"Then the angel said to her, 'Do not be afraid, Mary, for you have found favor with God... And behold, you will conceive in your womb and bring forth a Son, and shall call His name Jesus.'"

Mary and the angel engaged in a full conversation in which she could hear and see the angel, Gabriel.

This encounter announced the pregnancy, name, and the mission of the King of Kings.

The communication is never delivered or identified in the form of a dream or vision. Sometimes an encounter and a vision is interchangeable. Such was the case with Saul, later know as Paul.

"As he journeyed, he came near Damascus, and suddenly a light shone around him from heaven. Then he fell to the ground, and heard a voice saying to him, 'Saul, Saul why are you persecuting me?'"

Saul was knocked off his horse by a divine light while listening to a voice giving him instruction. Paul experienced a vision/encounter that transformed his life. Many people claim to have experienced supernatural encounters. I'm often asked if I believe in aliens. My answer is, "Of course I do, they are called Angels!"—demonic or divine.

Mary experienced the greatest encounter ever recorded by humanity.

I had the privilege of playing drums with one of the greatest bands ever assembled in the 20th century, *Earth, Wind and Fire*. It was around 1994. I was playing drums in the first of a five-day rehearsal schedule. During a break I was introduced to Maurice White, the architect, writer, lead singer and percussionist of the band. He was sitting in the back of the rehearsal studio in Burbank, California called Third Encore Rehearsal Studios. The lead singer, Phillip Bailey, introduced me to Maurice White. Among the few questions I posed to him, I asked Mr. White how he came up with the name Earth, Wind and Fire. He said, "I had a vision and saw the elements—earth, wind and fire." After that conversation, my life was radically changed.

My first performance with EWF was in Brunei, performing for the nephew of the Sultan of Brunei. While touring, I had a chance to visit one of the castles. I remember feeling overwhelmed while looking out of the castle's window. I heard a voice say, "Now that you have seen all the world has to offer will you preach for me." That was the first of a series of encounters, visions and dreams on that life-changing journey of my life.

Encounters are often life-changing—especially when we are open to them.

The apostle Paul's life was never the same after the vision/encounter on the Road to Damascus.

Keep in mind, encounters can also be Demonic. Such was the case with the first King of the Children of Israel, Saul. After Saul lost his mind and his sense of purpose, he sought after a dark medium (witch). "Then Saul said to his servants, 'Find me a woman who is a medium that I may go to her and inquire of her.'" Saul was no longer receiving mail of any form from heaven. Feeling desperate, Saul sought out a medium.

"So Saul disguised himself and then came to the woman by night." It doesn't take a genius to figure this out. The most powerful man of Israel had to disguise himself and sneak out to seek a Séance. This is all Dark!

"Please conduct a séance for me and bring up for me, the one I shall name for you."

A séance is when people make contact with the dead. King Saul goes against all he knew according to God's law. God is not the God of the dead, but the God of the living.

I'm not here to preach to you. You can read the rest of the story and witness the outcome for yourself.

Make sure you pay attention to your motives and the source of any encounter you experience.

My Greatest Encounter

I would like to share with you the Greatest Encounter of My Life. It was 1993, I was a musician, struggling spiritually and emotionally. I felt like every step I took forward in my music career; my character issues would take me two steps backward. I moved to Los Angeles to pursue my dreams of becoming a great drummer. I was attending West Angeles Church of God in Christ in Los Angeles where Bishop Charles E. Blake was Pastor. Spiritually, I was literally in a fight for my life. I was always well aware of

VISIONS

my gift as a gifted seer through dreams and visions. So why was I struggling I thought.

One Wednesday evening, August 4, 1993, I attended a session at our church called, "The Prayer and Bible Band". I heard the leader, Mother Ernestine Stephens, who recently passed, say, "These kind only come out by prayer and fasting." When I heard those words, something spoke to me and said, "Go on a three day fast with no food and just water."

I had never done a fast of any kind, and I was thirty years old at the time. I was desperate for relief and seeking an encounter with God. I wanted God to absolutely reveal Himself to me.

I attended church most of my life. I prayed, read the Bible, and played music in the church. But I was not spirit-filled or spirit-led. I absolutely wanted that experience. So, I decided I would go on a three day fast at the very moment I heard Mother Stephens share those words.

I discovered the church was having an "all night shut-in" starting the following Thursday night. A shut-in is when you attend a prayer service that takes place all night. In 1993, West Angeles' mid-week service was on Thursday nights. The shut-in took place immediately after service and would last until 6:00 a.m. on Friday morning. It was led by a wonderful woman they called Mother Maynard and Elder John Taylor. Elder Taylor later became a spiritual staple in my life.

So, I attended a shut-in for the first time in my life, and it was amazing. The shut-in resumed Friday night at 6:00 p.m. on August 6, 1993. I was totally in a surrendered state of mind. During this period of surrender between Wednesday and Friday night, I was divinely instructed to exercise many acts of Faith. It was like a voice challenging me in my head. I almost gave up fasting on Friday morning. I recall sharing with my mechanic's wife that I was struggling to continue my fast. She recommended that I read a book entitled, *Help, The Devil Wants Me Fat*. It was a book on fasting and exactly what I needed in that moment.

I will never forget that life-changing experience as long as I live. On Friday night, August 6, 1993, I was given one final spiritual instruction in my mind. The voice instructed me to say these words to a woman who was on her knees praying. Ironically, I ran into this woman just two weeks ago in 2024. I had not seen or spoken to her since that Friday night 32 years ago. I looked at her, and she looked at me and we both asked at the same time, "Where do I know you from?" After a series of questions, I asked her if she had ever attended West Angeles Church. Her reply was, "Yes." The more I looked in her eyes and heard her voice I realized she was the woman from the shut-in in 1993. She remembered, and we both hugged each other in utter amazement. I always wanted to know her name. Her name is Sonja Houchens. The words I was told to share with her were, "Please let me know when I get filled with the Spirit." She said, "Okay!" Keep in mind, I didn't know Sonja at the time, so this was a step of Faith.

She was on her knees when I made the request, and I got up from where she was and went on the steps of the altar and began praying. I raised my hands and began yelling at the top of my voice, "Hallelujah, Hallelujah!" over and over again. You see, at that time, I had so much shame and pride I felt I wasn't good enough for God. I grew up teasing and making fun of people in church who claimed they were filled with the Spirit, spoke in tongues and danced around the church. Yet, there I was fighting for my spiritual life.

While at the altar on my knees, eyes closed, hands raised I could hear people talking. I heard a male voice saying to someone, "Pray for him." They began laying hands on me and I could feel my body literally raising up from the floor.

I was finally filled with God's Spirit. "It actually happened!" I thought. The woman, Sonja Houchens, whom the Spirit instructed me to document my experience before it happened, said to me, "You will become a spiritual general."

When I awakened from the experience, I was lying on the floor and Elder John Taylor was patting my hand when I came to. I had peace beyond all my understanding. Many days later, people would tell me that I had a halo over my head. Even my own brother Nick Belle said I had a halo over my head. I would look in the mirror for the halo over my head and never saw it. One day while walking down the hallway at West Angeles Church, Bishop Blake walked up to me and said, "Hey, I heard you got a good dose." He said other encouraging words and then went into his office. Before the door closed he came back out, took my hand, looked me right in the eyes and said, "You are a good drummer but a great man," and went back to his office.

I can only share my own experience. This wasn't just any experience; it was a divine encounter that reshaped everything about my life.

VISIONS

Everything wasn't perfect from that day forward, however, I absolutely knew and know that God and His Spirit is real. God personally revealed Himself to me. I call this my Damascus experience. I recommend everyone should have that experience. The encounter destroyed every doubt I had about God.

Your encounter may be different from mine. Whatever it was you don't need the validation of others to validate it. If you haven't experienced a divine visitation, you can simply ask like I did. My relationship with God is the most important interaction of my life. As a result of that experience, all my gifts began to manifest—such as writing, music arrangement, speaking, producing, and publishing. I'm exercising gifts and talents that I never imagined.

You have the same Spiritual DNA as God. You can exercise all your gifts and walk in your creative purpose today. If you are not exercising all of your gifts, just surrender your life to Him. Build your own relationship with God and He will reveal Himself to you. You were literally created to manifest God's nature.

CHAPTER THREE

MEDITATION

Meditation is a practice that involves training the mind to achieve a state of calmness, focus and awareness. It involves directing attention to a specific object, thought, or sensation while letting go of distractions and judgements.

Meditation can be practiced in various ways, including:

- **Mindfulness meditation**: Focusing on the breath or bodily sensations
- **Guided Meditation**: Following instructions from a teacher or recording.
- **Mantra Meditation**: Repeating a word or phrase.
- **Visualization Meditation**: Creating a mental image of peaceful, calming scenes

Benefits of Meditation:

- Reduced stress and anxiety
- Improved sleep
- Increased focus and concentration
- Boosted immune system
- Reduced pain
- Improved overall-being

Meditation is a slow, long-term exercise that reorganizes the mind over months and years. It can slowly resolve conflicting patterns, optimize distraction filters, and strengthen focus.

In meditation, you hold an intention. For example, focus on your breath, because your mind will keep interrupting your attention with thoughts, sensations, drowsiness, and various emotions. You cannot consciously prevent those distractions. All you can do is return to your intention each time you realize you are distracted and trust your mind to slowly transform.

Through meditation, we can clear our minds of trauma, stress, pain, depression, desperation, and negative energy.

With divine writing tools of meditation, we can create a world of peace, love, healing, restoration, and endless dreams and visions.

The distinction between mental and spiritual meditation depends on the individual's intent and the specific technique.

As you can see, meditation supports our physical and mental well-being. But meditation is much, much more. Meditation has spiritual benefits as well as mental.

Is Meditation a Sin?

The practice of meditation is older than all books, especially religious ones. So, no—meditation is not inherently a sin. The practice is encouraged in several religions, including Judaism, Christianity, and Islam.

Various forms of meditation exist. While Christian meditation centers on God's Word and presence, other forms may be viewed as problematic if they focus on anything that conflict with a particular faith or doctrine.

What Does the Bible Say About Meditation?

The Bible encourages meditation on God's Word, Law, and works. Scripture prescribes meditation of God's Word day and night. God instructs Joshua to meditate on His Word to build courage as he lead the Children of Israel to the Promised Land.

"After the death of Moses the servant of the Lord, it came to pass that the Lord spoke to Joshua the son of Nun, Moses' assistant, saying: 'Arise,

MEDITATION

go over this Jordan, you and all this people, to the land which I am giving to them the Children of Israel.'"

As you can see, God spoke directly to Joshua and armed him with the weapon of meditation.

"This book of the law shall not depart from your Mouth, but you shall meditate on in it Day and Night, that you may observe to do according to all that is written in it. For then you will make your way prosperous, and then you will have good success."

A life-long prescription for success involves meditation day and night.

The spiritual practice of meditation helps identify who, what, and why we meditate. God instructed Joshua to meditate on His Word. He was instructed to recite and meditate on the Word day and night.

Notice, as a result of Word affirmation and reciting Scripture, Joshua would be prosperous and have good success.

Meditation provides success and prosperity.

Clearly the practice of meditation is not a sin when exercised properly.

It's time to exercise your divine resources, including meditation. You should no longer be held hostage by chains of fear, ignorance, and religion. Meditation, like dreams and visions, is divine postage waiting to be delivered for your good success.

Let's observe the benefits of meditation according to David and Paul. These two giants of Scripture recommend meditation when struggling with anger.

David warns, "Be angry, and do not sin, meditate within your heart on your bed and be still." Further evidence that meditation is not evil or sinful when dealing with our emotions.

David said, "Be angry"—embrace the anger. Don't run from it, confront it. When he said, "Do not sin," his warning is not to act on your emotions, but to meditate. Meditation requires you to stop and think. David said to "meditate within your heart." The heart is the core of our being.

Control Center: The heart acts as the spiritual and moral compass, determining one's direction and behavior in life.

Reflection: The instruction to meditate within your heart encourages quiet, personal introspection.

Self-examination: It involves searching for your inner motivations and feelings rather than acting out of anger. We should seek a connection to wisdom and God's guidance.

Paul gives similar advice as it relates to monitoring anger: "Be angry, and do not sin. Do not let the sun go down on your wrath."

Have your moment of anger, but don't allow anger to rule the day. Don't act on it with unhealthy behavior—respond to anger with meditation.

Meditation is a resource tool that God clearly recommends when dealing with anger and rage. Anger impacts the body, soul and spirit.

How Do I Get Started?

Initially, meditation was hard for me to practice. Just the thought of being still and thinking about nothing was quite challenging. However, today I utilize the supernatural tool of meditation more and more. Meditation is one of the reasons I decided to write this book.

The church has often portrayed meditation as something spooky and demonic. Nothing could be further from the truth. This is like leaving property—or unclaimed resources—to complete strangers.

If anyone should enjoy the wealth of meditation, it should be a child of God.

I would like to share with you meditation steps from my meditation counselor and friend, Deloise Maddox. Mrs. Maddox, who has practiced daily meditation for over fifty years, is also the author of *People Over Eighty*.

Meditation as a Daily Practice

Deloise Maddox

Introduction: Meditation is an active practice of training your attention and awareness to achieve a mentally clear and emotional calm state. It involves focusing on your breath and provides benefits such as reduced stress, improved focus, and emotional well-being. It is best supported by a quiet, still environment.

MEDITATION

The process of meditation has been my daily appointment with God, the higher intelligence, for over 50 years. I personally use mindfulness meditation, which focuses on the breath and being present in the moment.

How to practice meditation:

1. Find a comfortable posture. Sit upright with a tall frame, remain relaxed, keep your feet flat on the floor, and place your hands on your lap with palms facing up.
2. Focus your attention. Direct your attention to a single point, such as your breath.
3. Acknowledge wandering thoughts. When your mind drifts, gently acknowledge the thought without judgment and guide your attention back to your breath. To maintain focus, concentrate on the breath.
4. Be present. Aim to stay aware of the present moment, allowing thoughts and feelings to come and go without getting caught up in them.
5. Listen without judgment to ideas, thoughts, and visions that come through during this silent, sacred time.

Benefits of Meditation: As a result of over 50 years of daily meditation, I have experienced the following benefits:

- Increased awareness of my own thoughts and feelings
- Strengthened my ability to stay focused and resist distractions
- Developed greater emotional stability and a more positive outlook on life
- Mental clarity and daily problem solving
- An internal communication system for creative visioning and manifestation
- Calmness and peace in the body and mind, allowing one to manifest unconditional love, generosity, gratitude, and freedom from internal influences that disrupt focus and self-control
- A systematic approach to building positive relationships with family, friends, business associates, and multicultural and international individuals

In summary, practicing daily meditation facilitates becoming an ambassador who expresses compassion and collaborative service for humanity.

Meditation provides direct access to the Divine Postmaster, God. Meditation is the supernatural window to heaven. Meditation is one's divine canvas used to capture the creation of ideas, dreams, and visions through the instrument of imagination.

Dreams, visions, and meditation are unstoppable weapons of success. These divine resources of creativity are always at your disposal. Don't be afraid to be different. Don't limit yourself to terrestrial resources only. Your Divine Postmaster has awarded you unlimited capacity through the inherited spiritual gift of meditation.

I must say, adding meditation to my arsenal of creativity has absolutely changed my life. I can affirm that it has provided a greater level of peace, focus and success. I started meditating for one minute a day, and now I'm up to five to twenty minutes. My goal is to meditate a minimum of thirty minutes a day, at least five days a week.

Meditation was clearly the missing piece—naturally, emotionally, and spiritually. I will forever be a student of meditation. Thank you so much, Deloise Maddox, for sharing your guidance and gift of meditation with me and so many others. Mrs. Maddox meditates at a set time every day, so every time I meditate around that time, I'm constantly aware of my meditation ally.

Hopefully, I have put to rest some of your fears or apprehensions around meditation. Meditation is mentioned over 43 times in the Bible. Meditation is the building block of our dreams and visions. Meditation is the stamp on your divine mail waiting to be read.

The greatest divine trio ever assembled is dreams, visions and meditation. They are agents of creativity in all areas of life.

Meditation is the miracle of the moment.

CHAPTER FOUR

ARE YOU A GIFTED DREAMER?

A **Gifted Dreamer** is a frequent dreamer whose dreams have meaning or come true. A gifted dreamer has the ability to communicate with the unseen realm through dream state. Gifted dreamers combine exceptional imagination with the ability to manifest ideas, engage in abstract thinking, and carry a strong vision for goals—often linked to spiritual sensitivity.

A **Gifted Dream Interpreter** is someone born with the ability and skill to interpret dreams accurately. For example, prophets are uniquely gifted with the ability to interpret dreams.

Spiritually, gifted dreamers are categorized as lucid. Gifted dreamers are aware they are dreaming and can potentially influence the dream content. A lucid dream state allows for a unique experience in which the dreamer can consciously interact with the dream world.

Keep in mind, everyone has access to Dream Language, and everyone experiences some type of dream state. The difference between a frequent dreamer and a gifted dreamer is that the gifted dreamer's dreams carry significance.

The wisest man who ever lived, Solomon, spoke about frequent dreamers: "For a dream comes through much activity, and a fool's voice is known by his many words, for in the multitude of dreams and many words there is also vanity."

DREAM INTERPRETATION

Multitude of dreams…word…vanity! A possible translation, "For many useless things and words (come) in an abundance of dreams." Most dreams have little meaning—this is not the case for the gifted dreamer.

Don't confuse a Dream Interpreter with a Gifted Dreamer. These are two different skill sets.

As a child, I experienced many dream states. During that period of my life, most of my dreams were not positive because many of them were nightmares. I often woke up afraid. I recall wetting the bed until I was nine years old, probably because I was too afraid to go to the bathroom. Growing up, we shared a home with many uninvited insects and animals. I was just as afraid of my natural environment as I was of my dark dream state. Nightmares are not the best introduction for children who dream.

Nightmares—also known as bad dreams—are unpleasant dreams that can trigger powerful emotional responses such as fear, terror, and depression. Nightmares can be caused by stress, death, anxiety, trauma, unresolved issues, or lack of sleep. Sometimes they are linked to mental health conditions. Nightmares, like pain, alert us to psychological or spiritual issues that need to be addressed. As you can see, even nightmares can be positive indicators.

I remember waking from nightmares as a six-year-old child. I can still recall living in St. Louis, Missouri, in a two-family flat unit at 1232-A Walton Street. The A unit was upstairs.

Not only did I experience nightmares, but I also sleepwalked. Once, while in dream state, I walked down the street and woke up terrified, holding onto a fence while screaming—wondering how I had gotten outside. I firmly believe many of those dreadful nightmares were dark and demonic attacks. I believe it is important to pray with our children before sleep and to pray over them during sleep. My nightmares, however, were still part of my dream skill development.

As I grew older, my dreams became more pleasant, puzzling, and fascinating. I noticed many of my dreams provided warnings, direction, and expression—and most importantly, they came true. I realized I was a gifted dreamer, so I began paying closer attention to my dreams and visions.

One day in high school, my teacher called my name to bring me back to the classroom because I was so deep in daydreaming. Many of those daydreams came true.

I began paying serious attention to my dreams in my twenties. Today, there is much more information available about dreams and visions than there was back then. Honestly, I can only attest to my experience as a gifted dreamer.

My dream skill came into focus when I began writing my dreams down. I once heard someone say that if you write all your dreams down and date them, you can see your life coming together like a puzzle.

Gifted Dream Interpreter

Again, don't confuse a gifted dreamer with a gifted dream interpreter. A dream interpreter can accurately determine the meaning of a dream. As mentioned earlier, a gifted dream interpreter is born with the skill and ability to interpret dreams.

The greatest dream interpreters in Scripture were Joseph and Daniel. These gifted interpreters saved lives and altered history. Many leaders throughout history have relied on dream interpreters to make major decisions.

Dream interpretation is truly a God-given gift. Dream interpreters not only interpret their own dreams but accurately interpret the dreams of others.

As mentioned in Chapter Two, when I was filled with God's Spirit—a life-changing encounter—my life became supernaturally charged. Everything I touched, saw, and felt was intensified. One area that was especially intensified was my ability to interpret dreams.

I noticed how focused and accurate I was when interpreting my own dreams and the dreams of others. I began sharing my dreams publicly and explaining how they came true. People started calling me regularly to interpret their dreams. The more dreams I interpreted, the sharper my interpretation skills became.

I realized I had a genuine, God-given gift of dream interpretation.

For me, dream interpretation is an untrained skill—an ability I exercise naturally. Like any gift or talent, it still requires study and refinement. I began comparing and studying other gifted dream interpreters, keeping in mind the scripture that says, "David played skillfully." Skill requires practice and experience.

DREAM INTERPRETATION

I firmly believe there is a distinction between a gifted person and a talented person, even though the words are often used interchangeably. Gifts are bestowed from heaven; talents are acquired or learned.

I was born a gifted drummer. I never had a drum lesson for most of my life. When my great-aunt, Isabella Hughes, mailed my first set of drums through the JCPenny catalog at age eleven, my mother and I took them to church. I immediately began playing. My mother jumped up and ran out of the church because she knew I had never taken a lesson.

Our gifts originate in heaven from the Gift Giver. We refine them through life experiences, practice, and learning. Don't confuse education with learning. You don't need formal education or a traditional teacher to express or perfect your gift.

The more I played the drums, the better I became. The more I exercised my talent, the more opportunities appeared. The same is true of my gift of dream interpretation—the more I exercise it, the better I get.

You don't have to prove to anyone you are a gifted dreamer or dream interpreter. Your gift will validate itself. At times, I felt strange having the gift of dream interpretation. There aren't many people walking around announcing they interpret dreams. Yet, as I continued exercising my gift, its authenticity became undeniable.

Today, I am writing my second book on dreams and visions. If I can do it, you can too. Gifts are expressions from God. You don't need anyone to verify or validate what God has uniquely created within you.

Whatever your gift is, the world awaits your contribution. "A man's gift makes room for him and brings him before great men."

The Master Prophet said, "Whatever you ask in my name I will do."

Your gift of dream interpretation did not come from Santa Claus, family, friends or loved ones. Your divine postage came from heaven—from the Master Creator. If the Master has empowered you with the gifts of dreams and dream interpretation, it is up to you to exercise those gifts for His designed purpose in your life.

Review

- The gifts of dreams and dream interpretation come from heaven.
- You do not need a degree or validation from anyone to exercise your dream gift.

ARE YOU A GIFTED DREAMER?

- Do not confuse a gifted dreamer with a dream interpreter. Gifted dreamers experience frequent dreams that have significance and come true.
- Dream interpreters provide accurate meaning and understanding.

So—are you a Gifted Dreamer or a Dream Interpreter?

CHAPTER FIVE

DREAM INTERPRETATION

Generally, Dreams are motivated from self, darkness or God. What good is a letter or correspondence if you cannot understand the language? Spiritual postage is no different. What good are dreams if we can't understand them?

Most dream letters are written in symbols. Images, sounds, and words make up dream language. It's important to pay attention to your own unique dream language. Some people develop their dream language over time through experience. Others utilize tools as ChatGPT, Google, social media, books, and other resources to help interpret dreams.

Many people seek skilled or spiritual individuals to help interpret their dreams. Everyone dreams or communicates at some point through the medium of dreams and visions.

Most dream alphabet symbols are universal—numbers, colors, sounds, people, places, feelings, nature, family, animals, and objects, just to name a few. These timeless symbols transcend space, time, history, cultures, and religion.

First, interpretation begins by identifying the source or purpose of the dream. Who is attempting to communicate with you, and why? Determining the purpose of the dream helps clarify whether it has any significance—and if it does, what the dream is communicating.

Second, once the significance of the dream is established, you want to understand the purpose of the dream correspondence.

DREAM INTERPRETATION

Third, what is the interpretation? Interpreting a dream is like reading a letter written specifically to you. The difference between natural and supernatural correspondence is the mail carrier. Like Amazon, UPS, and the United States Postal Service, it's important to identify who is delivering your mail.

Natural mail carriers are human; supernatural mail carriers are spiritual. Familiarize yourself not only with spiritual mail but with spiritual mail carriers. These carriers travel through dimensions of time and eternity.

I often receive spiritual downloads in the morning when I'm in the shower. You don't have to be asleep to receive communication from the spiritual realm. Pay attention to where and when you encounter spiritual downloads. Your conditioned instincts will alert you to an impending download.

I am not a licensed, educated or certified dream interpreter. I am, however, a gifted dream interpreter. Over the years, I have had the pleasure of interpreting thousands of dreams. I can only share my experiences and testimonies.

I have observed that dreams with significance usually have a purpose or goal. When interpreting dreams, look for that purpose. Significant dreams often convey warnings, guidance, inspiration, comfort, resolution, confirmation, instructions involving life and death, or answers to prayers and petitions.

Other than God, there is no absolute universal authority on dream interpretation. Like law, medicine, and other professions, dream interpretation is a practice. The most reliable source for dream interpretation is God. God created the dreamer, the medium, the carrier, the messenger, and the interpreter.

I recommend God—the architect and creator of communication and expression. Dream interpretation is a powerful and timeless skill available to everyone, whether rich or poor, educated or uneducated, male or female—especially when God is your first option.

Language did not begin on earth with humanity, and neither did dream language. The divine alphabet originates in heaven.

One of the most powerful languages in heaven and on earth is music. Music is a divine language that needs no interpretation. If there is music or instrumentation in your dreams, pay attention to how it makes you feel during the dream and when you awaken.

DREAM INTERPRETATION

Music activates both the left and right sides of the brain. The left side processes language, while the right side processes melody and rhythm.

Music is often called the food of the soul because it originates in heaven. On earth, sound travels at approximately 761 miles per hour. Sound requires a medium to travel through—air. Sound and air are partners; music and spirit are partners. Music is an energized force of life.

Sound through music is a universal language in heaven and on earth—spoken by God, angels and all creation. Musical dictation is expressed through symbols called notes.

Joseph—The Gifted Dream Interpreter

Pharaoh was an Egyptian ruler who had a dream that no one in his cabinet could interpret. As a last hope, Pharaoh summoned Joseph, an imprisoned dream interpreter. As mentioned earlier, the best interpreter of dreams and visions is God. Listen to what Joseph said to Pharaoh:

"Pharaoh said to Joseph, 'I have had a dream, and there is no one who can interpret it. But I have heard it said of you that you can understand a dream, to interpret it.' So, Joseph answered Pharaoh saying, 'It is not me; God will give Pharaoh an answer of peace.'"

Joseph gave credit to God. There is no record of Joseph receiving formal training in dream interpretation. At age seventeen, he began sharing his dreams with his family, who rejected both him and his dreams. Nevertheless, Joseph continued to honor God, and God him in every circumstance.

When you are in close proximity to a favored dream interpreter, you also gain access to divine favor. God chooses gifted dreamers at His discretion. The dreamer and the interpreter are favored and protected by God. Be cautious how you handle God's property.

Another great dream interpreter was Daniel. He was sought out after King Nebuchadnezzar could not find anyone to interpret his dream.

After the king's wise men, musicians, astrologers, and enchanters failed, Daniel—a refugee slave on death row—was recommended.

"The king said to Daniel, 'Are you able to make known to me the dream which I have seen, and its interpretation?'"

"There is a God in heaven who reveals secrets, and He has made known to King Nebuchadnezzar what will be in the last days."

Two gifted dream interpreters whose lives seemed hopeless were rescued because they were skilled readers of divine mail.

Dream interpreters are life changers—not only for dream recipients, but for the interpreters themselves. The king rewarded Daniel greatly after the interpretation.

"Then the king promoted Daniel and gave him many great gifts; and he made him ruler over the whole province of Babylon, and chief administrator over all the wise men of Babylon."

Daniel and Joseph were promoted to the highest offices of government. Their interpretations saved lives and transformed kingdoms, nations, and enemies.

Not every dream carries the weight of Joseph's or Daniel's dreams. But when a dream is important, how you respond to your dream mail can be a matter of life and death.

How Can I Determine If the Dream Is From God?

You will know a dream is from God because you will not have peace until it is resolved. Your spirit will be unsettled, and the dream will speak to your core. Pharaoh and Nebuchadnezzar each had the same dream twice. Repeated dreams often demand revelation.

"How can I determine if the dream or dream interpreter is divinely inspired?" When the interpretation is divinely inspired, it is accurate, brings clarity, offers revelation, and gives God credit. God-inspired dream interpretation is empowered by the Spirit of God.

Generally, there are three dream interpretation options:

1. Ask God for the interpretation (prayer, meditation, Scripture)
2. Seek a gifted dream interpreter
3. Self-interpretation (collaboration with others)

Self-Interpretation Guidelines

1. Wake up
2. Write the dream down
3. Identify the theme

DREAM INTERPRETATION

4. Determine the dream's goal
5. Establish your dream language
6. Categorize the dream
7. Narrate the dream (who or what is communicating)
8. Create a dream journal

Dream interpretation is God's supernatural manual about you.

CHAPTER SIX

DREAM INTERPRETATION FORMULA

Dream interpretation is like reading a story, solving a mystery, or constructing a puzzle. Whatever the case, your dream mail is addressed to you. What makes dream mail different is the service and the carriers.

Dreams are dictated in the spiritual realm—the unseen environment. It's important to reduce your dreams to their lowest denominator, to their simplest form. Over time, you will become familiar with your own dream language and dialogue of exchange. Interpretation is not as complicated as you think if you follow a few communication guidelines.

Here are some dream interpretation guidelines.

1. What's the purpose or goal?
2. Who is the messenger?
3. Are you in the dream?
4. Origin of the message
5. Is this a repetitive dream? Prayer request or meditation?
6. Dream significance
7. Date and time of dream
8. Sounds, images and thoughts
9. Pay attention to symbols in the scene
10. Dream language

DREAM INTERPRETATION

Let's start with the messenger and the purpose of dreams.

Dreams from heaven are often easier to interpret because we have so many examples of dream interpretation in Scripture. The purpose of dreams from heaven is that you read and understand your divine letters. Like natural parents, they would not write you a letter you could not understand. Neither will God or His angels. God wants to communicate with you. His desire is to reveal His will and express His nature through you.

People often say the book of Revelation is complicated to understand. On the contrary, it's one of the least complicated books to understand in the Bible. Revelation contains an enormous amount of symbolism. The prophetic book communicates events throughout the ages—events of the past, (Roman history 2,000 years ago) the present (today) and the future (the end of time).

The Purpose of Revelation Is To Warn and Inspire Courage

The message and the messengers (mail carriers) are identified in Revelation Chapter One. "The Revelation of Jesus Christ, which God gave Him to show His servants things which must shortly take place. And He sent and signified it by his angels to His servant John."

The process is very clear. What did John do after experiencing the vision? He wrote the prophecy down. "Blessed is he who reads and those who hear the words of this prophecy and keep those things which are written in it."

Not only are the messenger and spiritual mail carriers identified, but the benefits of the message are established as well. Did you catch that?

Those who read, hear, and keep (do) the instructions of the messenger will be blessed. The goal of John's vision was clearly articulated. If you recall, the first two things you do after you have a dream are: 1) wake up, and 2) write the dream or vision down. That's what John did.

"Write the things which you have seen, and the things which are, and the things which will take place."

The message was not for John alone. He was the recipient of divine mail, and he was assigned to share the message with seven churches. "John, to the seven churches which are in Asia."

DREAM INTERPRETATION FORMULA

John followed the instructions revealed to him while he was a political prisoner on the Island of Patmos.

Dream and vision assignments from God are never subject to any negative circumstances you may be experiencing. Revelation was given to John while believers were enduring severe persecution. The prophecy was intended to provide encouragement in the midst of a dark period.

The first tools for interpreting dreams from heaven are prayer and Scripture. Allow Scripture to interpret Scripture. When downloading mail from the divine, natural tools are often ineffective.

"But the natural man does not receive the things of the Spirit of God, for they are foolishness to him: nor can he know them, because they are spiritually discerned." You cannot interpret light with darkness or mix evil with holiness.

Let's look at the word mystery and metaphorically apply the principles of mystery to understanding dream language.

Mystery: A novel, play, or movie dealing with a puzzling crime. Something unexplained or unknown. A secret, or the quality of being obscure or hard to understand.

Secret: Spiritual ceremonies or truths known only through faith or revelation. Something kept hidden or unexplained.

How to Solve Mysteries

Start by observing the scene. Ask questions and gather information by taking notes, mapping timelines, and identifying potential motives and clues. Finally, analyze the evidence, look for patterns, and collaborate with others to test theories until you identify the solution.

The Bible gives us simple clues when interpreting dreams from heaven. For example, the number zero often symbolizes miracles.

"The earth was without form, and void; and darkness was on the face of the deep." "Then God said, 'Let there be light.'"

The Creator began mapping out the seven-day building process, starting with zero. Out of nothing, God spoke everything into existence. The difference between God and human creation is that God begins with zero material, while man creates with some type of seen or unseen matter.

The number 4 symbolizes an appointed time. For example, there are four directions: north, south, east, and west. It rained forty days and forty nights. Jesus and Moses were in the wilderness forty days and forty nights. There are four seasons: summer, winter, spring, and fall.

The number 7 symbolizes completeness. In John's prophecy, there were seven angels, seven letters, seven churches, and seven years of tribulation revealed.

Angels are often used in scripture—Gabriel, Michael, and unidentified individuals who appear as angels. "Do not forget to entertain strangers, for by so doing, some have unwittingly entertained angels."

God also reveals Himself through nature: the rainbow, the stars, and creation itself. Jesus used birds and lilies to teach about God. Nature is the tangible expression of God. "For since the creation of the world, His invisible attributes are clearly seen."

Water represents Spirit. Jesus offers living water representing eternal life and the Holy Spirit. God also uses animals as symbolic messengers in dreams and visions: snakes, sheep, horses, lions, birds, and fish. Insects often symbolize judgment.

As you can see, there are many symbols you can compare in Scripture when seeking dream interpretation from heaven.

If dreams don't originate from heaven and you want to interpret them with others, there are additional resources available—such as gifted dream interpreters—or you can follow the guidelines I suggested.

Applying Puzzle Solving Principles to Dream Interpretation

Puzzle: A game, toy, or problem designed to test ingenuity or knowledge. A person or thing that is difficult to understand or explain—an enigma.

How to solve puzzles: Start by sorting pieces by color, pattern, and shape, and assemble the outer frame. Then break the remaining pieces into smaller, manageable sections and work one area at a time until the puzzle is complete.

Most dreams are like puzzles. I often use this approach more when dreams are not divine or of personal interest.

Notice the puzzle solving technique includes "solving problems designed to test." Sometimes dreams, for whatever reason, are designed or appointed to test some area of your life—naturally or spiritually. In life, we are always being tested. Dreams and visions can also serve as mediums for testing.

The puzzle-solving technique suggests putting together the frame first. In dream interpretation, identifying the structure and frame of the dream is also important. Simplify the smaller components so you can understand familiar people, places, and symbols. Then fill in the pieces you may not recognize. When you are finished, the picture of the dream should become clearer.

We've all heard the saying, "A picture is worth a thousand words." So are dreams and visions. Once you get a picture of the dream message, it will speak for itself—especially if it is a portrait of purpose.

How I Interpret Dreams

As a gifted dream interpreter, I interpret dreams—and life—with the formula of who, what, when, where, and why:

1. Who is the dream about?
2. What (subject/theme)?
3. When (time period in and out of the dream)?
4. Where (where is the dream or scene taking place)?
5. Why (purpose or goal)?

Like Joseph and Daniel, my process begins with prayer. I ask God for the interpretation. Then I ask the dreamer to write the dream exactly as it happened. They should include every detail they can remember, even if it doesn't make sense. Then I read the dream and make notes using the interpretation tools I've shared.

Dream language is very important. I try to identify the narrator, if there is one. Sometimes the narrator is the dreamer. Other times, the symbols and clues act as the narrator—colors, sounds, shapes, or just the scene itself.

People often tell me they don't dream or they can't remember their dreams. Everyone dreams, and everyone remembers their dreams. After I review the dream with the client, they usually realize they remember more than they thought.

DREAM INTERPRETATION

Once, a woman shared at a public dream session I conducted in July 2025 in Los Angeles, California, that she could not remember her dreams. I asked her how she felt when she woke up. She said, "Anxious and afraid." Those feelings were an extension of her dream state. We document dreams through our senses—one of those senses is feeling. So she realized she did remember. If she didn't remember her dreams, she could not have retained what she felt.

Dreams are also structured like songs and musical arrangements. They contain an introduction, verse, melody, chorus, bridge, vamp, and ending.

The message is in the melody. The melody is the most memorable part of the song. We often find ourselves humming the tune over and over again. That's how dream retention works. There's a part of the dream that stands out, and we replay it in our minds. In music, that repetitive melody is called a hook. Pay attention to the hook when interpreting your dreams.

What's the melody of your dreams? What keeps showing up over and over in your dream state? That is usually the message.

So often, a song or piece of music is inspired by someone or an event. Only the composer, writer, or lyricist knows the true motive. The same holds true for dreams and visions. Who—or what—is inspiring your dream and vision? Like music, if you listen, watch, and read the credits, the interpretation will reveal itself.

Art, songs, music, stories, films, books, and more are made available to the public through distributors. In the supernatural marketplace, dreams and visions function as distributors.

I would like to share with you a dream I interpreted for a gentleman we will call Mr. M. He texted his dream to me in November 2025. I interpreted his dream yesterday, Thursday, November 20, 2025, while having lunch at Bloom Cafe in Los Angeles, CA.

Here is Mr. M's Dream:

> Last night, I had this dream in which we were somewhere doing a play of sorts that was on a table. The table had two sides, and it seemed like we were all part of this play. Some people were saying, "Don't take this play too seriously," whereas the people participating in the play seemed to be taking it very seriously.

DREAM INTERPRETATION FORMULA

During the beginning of the play, I was trying to find a seat at the table, but there were no seats for me. Everyone was already sitting down and had established their spots, so I was thinking, Okay, where's my seat? I went around trying to find one — a wooden seat for the wooden table — and then I took a chair and sat down.

Then I saw that supposedly this character, a person named David — the name of the character I was supposed to play — was already being played by someone else. So I asked the person, "Hey, I'm supposed to be David, and it looks like you're David. Are there two Davids?" And he said, "Yeah, there are two Davids. I'm playing David on this side of the table; you're David on the other side of the table."

So I kept going and went to the other side of the table. I saw that, yes, there was a place for David, but still no seat. I brought my own chair and put it there. Then this person — kind of a woman-man mixture — who was leading the play gave me my lines. She said, "These are your lines," and the lines were: "I am your king. I will listen to your questions, and I will give you answers."

As soon as I got there, it was already my time to deliver the lines. I was still processing and hesitant because I didn't understand what was going on, but before I could say anything, she immediately went up and did the lines for me in front of everyone. I didn't like that — those were my lines. So I went up to the top of the table (there was no stage, just the table) and said, "No — I am your king. I will listen to your questions, and I will give you answers."

Then, in the next part of the dream, I was crouched down by a door, listening to these young people — they were young in the dream too — bringing me their questions. As they asked me questions, I would answer by asking them a question back. They all started to contemplate and meditate on the questions I asked because the answer was within the question.

Then I realized, in the next scene, that they were enacting all the answers I had given them. They were making body sculptures — groups of people forming images that represented the answers they discovered through the questions I had asked. I was

DREAM INTERPRETATION

in the center of their sculptures, and I realized that somehow, through the process, I had learned that this role was the role of King David from the Bible.

That was the role I had been given — the role of King David — and through the dream, I figured out that's who he was and what he did. I embodied it and did a good job with it.

Mr. M's Dream Interpretation: (I)

First Paragraph

D "The table had two sides"

I Each side of the table in Mr. M's dream are symbols and clues which represent his dream language and his inability to make decisions.

D "This play"

I The play represents the dream plot and Mr. M's gifts and profession. (In life he is a film writer and photographer.)

D "Don't take this play too seriously"

I Symbolizes the narrative or negative voices in the dreamer's head.

Second Paragraph

D "I was trying to find a seat at the table"

I "The table" symbolizes Mr. M's lifelong question about his place in life.

D "But there were no seats for me"

I Mr. M has to create his own seat (work for himself) in his Life. He doesn't have to depend on others.

D "Everyone was already sitting down and had established in their spots"

I Sitting down and established symbolize stability in the roles of other people within his profession.

D "I was thinking, 'Okay, where is my seat?'"

I "Where is my seat?" symbolizes his place in life.

DREAM INTERPRETATION FORMULA

D "I went around trying to find one."

I The seat represents his purpose and place in life.

D "A wooden seat for the wooden table, and then I took a chair and sat down."

I Wooden chair symbolizes unfinished business. The seat is not varnished, painted, or decorated. Mr. M should decorate (arrange) his life the way he sees it.

Third Paragraph

D "Then I saw that supposedly this character, a person named David."

I The character Mr. M saw was King David in the scriptures. King David symbolizes roles and challenges Mr. M will and has encountered in his life. The back and forth between a procrastinator or a person who should make decisions.

D "Was already being played by someone else."

I Reflects the dreamer's double personality, which Mr. M acknowledged.

D "Are there two Davids?"

I Which side of the table does Mr. M want to live on? Is he going to be a leader or a follower?

Fourth Paragraph

D "So I kept going and went to the other side of the table."

I Mr. M has to stay on the right side of the table and be himself.

D "Then this person, kind of a woman/man mixture who was leading the play gave me my lines."

I A woman in Mr. M's culture typically does not lead. A woman leading was contrary to his custom.

D She said, "These are your lines."

I "These are your lines" represents his opportunities in life.

DREAM INTERPRETATION

D "I am your king. I will listen to your questions, and I will give you answers."

I "I am your king" is Mr. M's affirmation that he has to be the king of his decisions!

Fifth Paragraph

D "As soon as I got there, it was already my time to deliver the lines."

I Mr. M has to seize the moment.

D "I was still processing and hesitant because I didn't understand what was going on."

I He was still procrastinating. He needs to decide. Procrastination symbolizes Mr. M's fears.

D "But before I could say anything, she immediately went up and did the lines for me in front of everyone."

I Mr. M missed his career opportunity designed just for him. Someone else read his lines and played his role. In real life, this keeps happening to him.

D "So I went up to the top of the table (there was no stage just a table)"

I "The stage" represents the characters that the dreamer plays in his real life. Because he struggles to make decisions, he continues to encounter missed opportunities, which leave him frustrated and confused.

D "No—I am your King. I will listen to your questions, and I will give you answers."

I Because it takes Mr. M so long to lead and make concrete decisions in various stages of his life, when he does speak, he's alone with no one listening. There are no characters, only negative voices in his head.

Sixth Paragraph

D "Then, in the next part of the dream, I was crouched down by a door, listening to these young people bringing me their questions."

DREAM INTERPRETATION FORMULA

I "Crouched down by the door" symbolizes his disappointment. "The young people" symbolize Mr. M's dreams and ambitions waiting to be fulfilled.

D "I would answer."

I Represents the positive affirming voices in Mr. M's head.

Seventh Paragraph

D "Then, I realized, in the next scene, that they were enacting all the answers I had given them."

I The word scene symbolizes moving on in the next chapter of Mr. M's life. Mr. M realizes, himself, he has all the creative resources to lead others in the next stages of his life. When he makes the decision to lead, others will model, follow, and copy his narrative.

D "I was in the center of their sculptures, and I realize that somehow, through the process I had learned that this role was the role of King David from the Bible."

I Mr. M learns people have been imitating and following him all along and he discovers he is actually a leader.

D "I had learned that this role was the role of King David from the Bible."

I Mr. M is to read the story of David in the Bible and study his process of becoming King. It's time he becomes the star of his own life productions.

Last Paragraph

D "That was the role I had been given—the role of King David."

I The role of King David symbolizes Mr. M's purpose. To exercise his gifts and purpose and take control of his destiny. To quote William Shakespeare, "All the world is a stage, and all the men and women merely players." Solomon, son of King David said, "A man's gift makes room for him and brings him before great men."

CHAPTER SEVEN

30-DAY DREAM INTERPRETATION JOURNAL

In keeping with what I call a divine outline of inspiration, documentation and verification, it's important that you document your dream interpretation journey.

For your convenience, I have provided a 30-Day Dream Interpretation Journal. Simply date and write your dreams on the front page. Then utilize my dream interpretation formula and write your interpretation on the back page.

The best way to become a better interpreter of your dreams is through practice. So, let's get started—it's time to read your mail!

DREAM INTERPRETATION

Dream   ___/___/___

Day 1

30-DAY DREAM INTERPRETATION JOURNAL

Interpretation

DREAM INTERPRETATION

Dream   ___/___/___

Day 2

30-DAY DREAM INTERPRETATION JOURNAL

Interpretation

DREAM INTERPRETATION

Dream   ___/___/___

Day 3

30-DAY DREAM INTERPRETATION JOURNAL

Interpretation

DREAM INTERPRETATION

Dream   ___/___/___

Day 4

30-DAY DREAM INTERPRETATION JOURNAL

Interpretation

DREAM INTERPRETATION

Dream ___/___/___

Day 5

30-DAY DREAM INTERPRETATION JOURNAL

Interpretation

DREAM INTERPRETATION

Dream ___/___/___

Day 6

30-DAY DREAM INTERPRETATION JOURNAL

Interpretation

DREAM INTERPRETATION

Dream   ___/___/___

Day 7

30-DAY DREAM INTERPRETATION JOURNAL

Interpretation

DREAM INTERPRETATION

Dream __/__/__

Day 8

30-DAY DREAM INTERPRETATION JOURNAL

Interpretation

DREAM INTERPRETATION

Dream ___/___/___

Day 9

30-DAY DREAM INTERPRETATION JOURNAL

Interpretation

DREAM INTERPRETATION

Dream ___/___/___

Day 10

30-DAY DREAM INTERPRETATION JOURNAL

Interpretation

DREAM INTERPRETATION

Dream   ___/___/___

Day 11

30-DAY DREAM INTERPRETATION JOURNAL

Interpretation

DREAM INTERPRETATION

Dream ___/___/___

Day 12

30-DAY DREAM INTERPRETATION JOURNAL

Interpretation

DREAM INTERPRETATION

Dream   ___/___/___

Day 13

30-DAY DREAM INTERPRETATION JOURNAL

Interpretation

DREAM INTERPRETATION

Dream ___/___/___

Day 14

30-DAY DREAM INTERPRETATION JOURNAL

Interpretation

DREAM INTERPRETATION

Dream   __/__/__

Day 15

30-DAY DREAM INTERPRETATION JOURNAL

Interpretation

DREAM INTERPRETATION

Dream ___/___/___

Day 16

30-DAY DREAM INTERPRETATION JOURNAL

Interpretation

DREAM INTERPRETATION

Dream ___/___/___

Day 17

30-DAY DREAM INTERPRETATION JOURNAL

Interpretation

DREAM INTERPRETATION

Dream ___/___/___

Day 18

30-DAY DREAM INTERPRETATION JOURNAL

Interpretation

DREAM INTERPRETATION

Dream   ___/___/___

Day 19

30-DAY DREAM INTERPRETATION JOURNAL

Interpretation

DREAM INTERPRETATION

Dream ___/___/___

Day 20

30-DAY DREAM INTERPRETATION JOURNAL

Interpretation

DREAM INTERPRETATION

Dream ___/___/___

Day 21

30-DAY DREAM INTERPRETATION JOURNAL

Interpretation

DREAM INTERPRETATION

Dream   ___/___/___

Day 22

30-DAY DREAM INTERPRETATION JOURNAL

Interpretation

DREAM INTERPRETATION

Dream ___/___/___

Day 23

30-DAY DREAM INTERPRETATION JOURNAL

Interpretation

DREAM INTERPRETATION

Dream ___/___/___

Day 24

30-DAY DREAM INTERPRETATION JOURNAL

Interpretation

DREAM INTERPRETATION

Dream ___/___/___

Day 25

30-DAY DREAM INTERPRETATION JOURNAL

Interpretation

DREAM INTERPRETATION

Dream ___/___/___

Day 26

30-DAY DREAM INTERPRETATION JOURNAL

Interpretation

DREAM INTERPRETATION

Dream ___/___/___

Day 27

30-DAY DREAM INTERPRETATION JOURNAL

Interpretation

DREAM INTERPRETATION

Dream ___/___/___

Day 28

30-DAY DREAM INTERPRETATION JOURNAL

Interpretation

DREAM INTERPRETATION

Dream ___/___/___

Day 29

30-DAY DREAM INTERPRETATION JOURNAL

Interpretation

DREAM INTERPRETATION

Dream ___/___/___

Day 30

30-DAY DREAM INTERPRETATION JOURNAL

Interpretation

Congratulations, welcome to the world of Dream Interpreter!

REFERENCES

New King James Version (NKJV), Thomas Nelson Publishers, 1982.

Earth, Wind and Fire (American Band), Formed by Maurice White, Chicago, Illinois, 1969.

Lovett, C.S., *Help Lord - The Devil Wants Me Fat!*, Personal Christianity, Middleton, Idaho, 1982.

Maddox, Deloise, *People Over Eighty*, Noahs Ark Publishing Service, Beverly Hills, California, (1st Publication 2018), 2025.

ChatGPT, (OpenAI), Founded by Sam Altman, Elon Musk, et al, San Francisco, California, 2015.

Google LLC, Founded by Larry Page and Sergey Brin as *Google Inc.*, Menlo Park, California, 1998.

Amazon.com, Inc. (DBA Amazon), Founded by Jeff Bezos as *Cadabra, Inc.*, Bellevue, Washington, 1994.

UPS (United Parcel Service, Inc.), Founded by James E. Casey as *American Messenger Company*, Seattle, Washington, 1907.

USPS (United States Postal Service), Agency Executive: David Steiner (Postmaster General), Washington, D.C., U.S., Formed 1971.

ALSO BY LAVAL W. BELLE

Your Gifts are Not Your Purpose

Your Dreams and Visions

Man How Many Children Do You Really Have?

For Speaking Engagements, Book Signings, Appearances, and Interviews,

Contact:
Noahs Ark Publishing Service
8549 Wilshire Blvd., Suite 1442
Beverly Hills, CA 90211

Phone:
(213) 884-8034

Email:
noahsarkpublishing@gmail.com

Website:
noahsarkpublishing.com

Made in the USA
Coppell, TX
21 February 2026

71930453R00069